Making Your First $100 Online

A step by step guide to starting your internet business.

IQ PRESS, INC.

Disclaimer

CONTENTS

Acknowledgments   i

1 Introduction   1

2 Getting started as an Affiliate   3

3 Choosing a Product to Promote   7

4 Your Hoplink   14

5 Marketing your Product with a Website   17

6 How Will People Find Your Site?   27

7 Conclusion   34

Reference Materials   36

ACKNOWLEDGMENTS

IQ Press, Inc. is a small publishing company dedicated to providing access to educational materials primarily in small business start-up and development. Their mission is to bring the reader useful information that can be implemented with a small capital outlay and generate income streams for the reader to implement.

We hope you enjoy these reports and that they will help improve your life.

www.IQPress.org

CHAPTER 1 - INTRODUCTION

"Making your first $100 online is easy..."

If you have surfed the web diligently, like me, in search of ways to make money online, you would have come across many videos with a caption like our opening statement in this guide – Making your first $100 online is easy...

Actually, it is easy to earn your first $100 online; you only need to know how to achieve it. Have you watched several videos online which did not yield any positive outcome? Welcome to the club! I watched hundreds of videos too, and found that most of them merely beat around the bush (though a few are quite helpful).

Notwithstanding, in this guide, you will learn a step by step method that will show you how to get started making your first $100 online. Very soon, you will join the league of those who are not just making $100, but have gone a step higher in earning more than a hundred bucks, daily.

The hardest part of making money generally is believing you can do it, and following through on the methods. Once you have successfully made your first $100 online, it becomes easier to earn more and more because your subconscious self-belief will help you build more confidence to earn much more, daily.

Really, making money online is not as hard as you think. Once you can overcome the first hurdle – believing; the amount of money you can make online becomes limitless. Everyone likes to see thousands of $$$ in their bank account and I bet you want that too.

A sure way to begin earning money is through affiliate marketing. It is a simple, easy to learn, less risky and precise way to earn some cool cash. Want to have some more money roll into your account this year? Follow the steps in this book as we explore how Affiliate marketing can help you earn a good income online.

Chapter 2 - Getting Started as an Affiliate

Affiliate marketing has changed the financial status of so many people. You may hear this and assume that it must be a difficult way of making money after all, but that isn't the case. It is pretty much the easiest way to make money that I have ever come across.

What we do in affiliate marketing, basically, is assist companies or individual merchants to sell their products by advertising for them and/or by referring people to their products. You don't have to create your own product in affiliate marketing, nor do you have to deal with customer service; you only have to look for an existing product to promote.

However profitable affiliate marketing might be, you still need the right platform to be able to achieve your financial goals. In this book, I will focus on Clickbank as an affiliate marketing platform.

What is Clickbank: you ask?

Clickbank is a top retailer of digital products. They do not deal with physical products – every product on Clickbank is digital and can only be downloaded.

Clickbank is probably the most used platform for affiliate marketing, and one may wonder why it is so. The reasons are not too complicated: Clickbank is super easy to use, the clients on this platform pay fat commissions, and their products make fast sales.

Therefore, I will use Clickbank to explain how to get started with affiliate marketing, even though there are other reputable affiliate companies like Paydotcom, Commission Junction and Pepperjam.

Getting Started on Clickbank

To get started as an affiliate marketer on Clickbank, follow the simple steps below:

• Visit www.clickbank.com to sign up.

• Click on the link that says "sign up" to create your own affiliate account

• Submit your physical address because Clickbank will use that to send you a check, via mail, for your commission (PayPal is currently not supported on the platform, but they have introduced a system that pays directly to your local bank account – very convenient for members outside the US).

• You will be required to include a nickname in your application. Your nickname will be attached to a link called Hoplink. It is through this link that Clickbank will track who they are to pay commission. (Note: be very discreet in choosing your nickname because customers can see it in the hoplink; moreover, it can't be changed at a later time)

How Does Clickbank Work?

Clickbank uses a very simple mode of operation. A merchant who has a digital product they want to sell will create it on Clickbank, then, an affiliate can view the details to see if he would like to take on the job.

If he is satisfied with the commission, which is usually between 50 - 75 percent for a merchant who is serious about sales, he will go ahead to promote the sales of the product. Most traders pay very high commissions because they are desperate to make sales.

Are you wondering why the commission is high? The affiliate does a lot of work in promoting the sales of a particular product. If the affiliate has to earn, then he must go the extra mile to ensure the product is sold. Oftentimes, the affiliate uses their personal funds to promote their sales campaign.

Trust me, all the trouble involved really deserves a high pay.

Perhaps you're curious as to a how a merchant creates their products – an eBook, a service or software. They simply submit it to Clickbank for verification and approval. Clickbank has a reputation for not accepting unfit products. By unfit, I mean illegal, fake and low-quality products.

This is one reason affiliate marketers can trust Clickbank. ☐

How Do Merchants Get Paid?

A merchant is paid depending on whether a buyer buys his product directly, or whether it is through an affiliate link. Irrespective of how a product or service is sold, Clickbank always takes 7.5 percent plus a $1 stocking fee, leaving 92.5 percent minus $1 to be shared between the merchant and the affiliate, if the product is purchased through an affiliate link.

If a buyer buys an item without an affiliate, the merchant gets 92.5 percent minus $1 stocking fee from the sale. However, if it is purchased through an affiliate link, Clickbank will pay the affiliate and the merchant, after removing its 7.5 percent + $1, based on the percentage the merchant set for the affiliate.

Confused?

Let's use a practical example here.

Assuming a merchant has an eBook that sells for $30. A buyer purchases it without an affiliate link. Here's a breakdown of what the merchant will get:

7.5 percent of $30 - $1 stocking fee (= $3.25) go to Clickbank

The merchant will get $30 - $2.25 - $1 stocking fee = $26.75

On the other hand, assume that the buyer purchases it through an affiliate link and that the merchant had set affiliate percentage to be 60 percent. The breakdown of what each will earn is shown below:

$3.25 goes to click bank

The affiliate will get 60 percent of $26.75 = $16.05

The merchant will have what is left which is = $10.70

I believe the illustration is clear enough, right?

I am sure that, by now, you are already getting excited to begin affiliate marketing on Clickbank. Just hold on, there's still more to unfold in the following chapters.

Chapter 3 - How to Choose a Clickbank Product to Promote?

Now that you have learned how payments are made to both the merchant and the affiliate, you need to learn how to choose a product to promote. When you visit www.clickbank.com on your web browser, you will see a link for "marketplace" as shown in the screenshot above.

If you have already signed up on Clickbank, just go ahead to click the link. Guess what? All of Clickbank's products will be displayed here.

If your internet is slow, you may want to grab a snack while you wait excitedly...

Clickbank's products are in different categories which include the following:

• Business to Business

• Health & Fitness

• Home & Family

• Computing & Internet

- Money & Employment

- Marketing & Ads

- Fun & Entertainment

- Sports & Recreation

- Society & Culture

If you are serious about affiliate marketing, I would advise you to click on each of the categories to have an idea of their uniqueness, as well as to find a product that may excite you.

Once you select a category, health & fitness for example, to check out, click on the "go" button at the bottom right hand side of the screen. You will then be taken to a list of all of the products in the health & fitness category.

Here's what the page looks like:

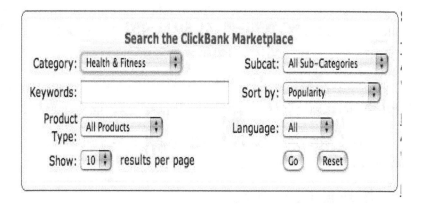

Clickbank always lists their products in the order of their popularity. Hence, the most popular products are usually at the top of the products page, while the least popular ones are far below.

Here is an example of the "health & fitness" product page.

(Take note of the first product on the page. I am going to use it to explain some must-know terms for everyone who wants to make money with affiliate marketing on Clickbank).

1) Fat Loss 4 Idiots. Affiliates: FatLoss4Idiots.com/aff :::: Thanks.
$/sale: $30.98 | Future $: - | Total $/sale: $30.98 | %/sale: 75.0% | %refd: 93.0% | grav: 609.76
view pitch page | create hoplink

2) Truth About Six-Pack Abs, Total Payouts Avg $30/sale W/rebills. New Trial Offer Has Exploded Conversions As Of March 9! Dont Worry, Lower Front Payouts At First, But You Receive The Full Commission At 21 Days. Go To Http://truthaboutabs.com/affiliate-info.html For The $30K/month Super-affil Strategies Newsletter.
$/sale: $24.14 | Future $: $22.27 | Total $/sale: $30.18 | %/sale: 75.0% | %refd: 91.0% | grav: 302.53
view pitch page | create hoplink

3) Top Secret Fat Loss Secret :: 75% Commission:: Best Affiliate Toolkit. Makes $25-$60 Per Sale | Converts As High As 3%-5% | We Tested Just 1 Promo & Made $2,280/24hrs | We Give You Same Promo Free! | Sells Itself! | Get 1st-Movers Advantage | Join Now Free! | Http://TopSecretFatLossSecret.com/affiliates.php.
$/sale: $32.20 | Future $: - | Total $/sale: $32.20 | %/sale: 75.0% | %refd: 92.0% | grav: 231.09
view pitch page | create hoplink

4) Chopper-Tattoo - Top Tattoo Offer ! The #1 Tattoo Gallery On The Web. Converting Like Crazy! Pays 75%, Affiliates Must See. Free Music Downloads With Membership Allows Creative Marketing. New Affiliate Tracking In Email, Exit Ad, & Google Upon Request: Chopper-tattoo.com/affiliates/.
$/sale: $20.17 | Future $: - | Total $/sale: $20.17 | %/sale: 75.0% | %refd: 95.0% | grav: 202.50
view pitch page | create hoplink

5) No Nonsense Muscle Building, Massive $73.48 & $52.67 Payouts. Write Your Own Paycheck With The Internets Highest Converting Muscle Building System! No One Comes Close. First Class Product With Superior Affiliate Support & Resource Center ...Too Many Tools To List! Http://www.vincedelmontefitness.com/affiliates.html.
$/sale: $54.76 | Future $: - | Total $/sale: $54.76 | %/sale: 75.0% | %refd: 75.0% | grav: 90.15
view pitch page | create hoplink

The product, Fat Loss 4 Idiots, is the most frequently downloaded diet plan for people that want to shed fat. This explains why it is first on the list. Using this product, let's now examine the symbols and values and what they mean. I am quite sure you've been wondering what they mean...

1) Fat Loss 4 Idiots. Affiliates: FatLoss4Idiots.com/aff :::: Thanks.
$/sale: $30.98 | Future $: - | Total $/sale: $30.98 | %/sale: 75.0% | %refd: 93.0% | grav: 609.76
view pitch page | create hoplink

"$/sale" refers to the average amount of money you will be paid per sale of this product, minus refunds. It is not always possible to predict how many customers, if any, will request for refunds in any given pay period.

"Future $" is applicable if a customer signs up for an ongoing subscription. The money derived from this subsription is what is written there. Therefore, a value of zero depicts that there is no subscription to the service. It is also called rebill revenue.

"Total $/sale" is the total amount that an affiliate will be paid for each sale, including all rebills too.

"%sale" simply shows the percentage of the sales price that goes to the affiliate. In the example of the product we are making reference to, 75 percent of the sales price go to the affiliate, which is quite common on Clickbank.

"%refd" helps to strike a contrast between a merchant's sales on Clickbank that were by affiliates and the ones that were not by affiliates. In the example we're considering, 93 percent of the merchant's sales are by affiliate links; whereas the merchant has only 7 percent to boast of.

(Practically, most merchants will make little or no money without affiliate marketers).

Here's what you can gain from that:

A high "%refd" means that affiliates really find the product very profitable to promote. On the other hand, a low value means that the merchant is doing pretty well on their own. Therefore, the choice will normally tend to the ones with a higher value, which is good.

"grav" is the short form for gravity. It shows how well a product sells on Clickbank. It is a value that gives an estimate of the total number of affiliates that helped to promote the product.

Wondering why it is decimal? There are also other factors that are considered by Clickbank to arrive at that value.

More often than not, affiliates tend to ignore products with a low "grav" value. In some cases, this may not be the best thing to do because there are products that may have not yet been explored by many affiliates but may have the potential of recording great sales.

In the same vein, a high "grav" value indicates that the market will most likely be congested with so many affiliates on the same product since it is a productive product. Consequently, it will be hard to make sales on such a product because many people are already promoting it.

To be on the safe side, I suggest that you choose a product with a gravity value that is neither too high nor too low – a product with moderate competition until you become a pro who can handle highly competitive markets.

Now that you know these terms, you can choose your preferred product, wisely and easily. After choosing your preferred product, click on "view pitch page" as shown in the picture below.

1) Fat Loss 4 Idiots. Affiliates: FatLoss4Idiots.com/aff :::: Thanks.
$/sale: $30.98 | Future $: - | Total $/sale: $30.98 | %/sale: 75.0% | %refd: 93.0% | grav: 609.76
view pitch page | create hoplink

Opening the pitch page is very important because it will help you know whether it is a product that should be promoted or not. Here are some things you can find on a pitch page:

•   A marketable (or, unfortunately, non-marketable pitch)

•   Details about the product

•   The merchant's description of the product as well as their emphasis of certain functions of the product

•   Testimonials from those who have bought and used the product.

•   You can also buy the product from here, which is a good idea as an affiliate, though it is not necessary to be able to promote it.

These, and a few other things, are what you will see on the pitch page.

About now, you should be clear on the right product to choose. However, there are just a few more things for you to note...

Okay, I know what you're thinking now: "Can't we get started already?" Am I right?

Well, you need to pick a product that works for you. Here's what I mean: Pick a product that you can relate to easily. Something that you are familiar with because it may be very frustrating trying to promote something that you do not know much about.

So, after analyzing the products and taking into consideration the above factors, ensure you pick a product that aligns with your personal interests.

Finally, be sure the product you pick is within the first and second product pages – every product outside that will probably be less sought after. (This is not a rule but an opinion).

With these, you won't have any problem picking the right product to promote. Let's move on to learning what a hoplink is in the next chapter.

Chapter 4 - Your Hoplink

The next thing to do after selecting your product is to create a hoplink. Don't panic, it will be explained shortly.

Your hoplink is a custom link that buyers will click to get access to the product page of the merchant you are advertising for. Therefore, to stand a better chance of getting more buyers, it is important you put your hoplinks on strategic platforms.

For example, you can place your link in email campaigns, and place it at the top, middle and bottom so that people reading your email campaigns won't eventually skip it. You can also place this link on your sales page, social media pages, and other platforms where you can draw people's attention to it.

Basically, a hoplink comprises your nickname (remember we set that at the beginning?), publisher's name and the words "hop.clickbank.net". Let's make it practical so you can understand it better.

Let's say your nickname is Salesguru, the merchant's name is charles, and then the words – hop.clickbank.net. Combining these three will give us an ideal hoplink. See the combination below:

https://salesguru.idiots.hop.clickbank.net

Creating Your Hoplink

Consider the image below, this should tell you that the first step is to open the product page. In the previous chapter, we clicked the view pitch page; however, in this chapter, we are going to click create hoplink

1) Fat Loss 4 Idiots. Affiliates: FatLoss4Idiots.com/aff :::: Thanks.
$/sale: $30.98 | Future $: - | Total $/sale: $30.98 | %/sale: 75.0% | %refd: 93.0% | grav: 60·
view pitch page | create hoplink

After clicking on that link, the window that appears will look like the image below:

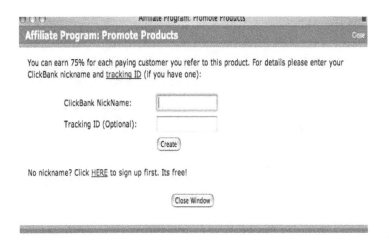

Then you will be required to fill in your Clickbank nickname and tracking ID (which can be up to eight characters – numbers or letters).

Although your tracking ID is optional, it may be useful in tracking where your sales come from so you can keep pitching the buyer for the same product or for other products. Keep tabs on the respective tracking ID and sales if you plan to use the information to promote products in the future.

IMPORTANT NOTICE!!! BE SURE YOUR NICKNAME IS SPELLED PROPERLY, OTHERWISE, YOUR SALES WON'T BE CREDITED TO YOUR ACCOUNT.

Chapter 5 – How to Market an Affiliate Product with a Website

This is perhaps the most important part of this book. Knowing how to create an affiliate account, how to choose an appropriate product and how to create a hoplink won't get you the money you want to earn. Rather, what will help you is how you are able to go about marketing the products.

Don't forget what our initial goal is – *how to make your first $100 online with affiliate marketing.*

If you want to get serious with affiliate marketing, there are some basic things you should do. They include:

•   Creating a web address which includes a sales page

•   Pitching the products with beautiful content and reviews on your sales page

•   Learning from the Experts

Let's get started with creating a sales page.

Obviously, you need a domain to get started. Visit godaddy.com to get your own domain now. It is advisable that the website name you choose should reflect the type of products you'd be promoting. For example, if you'll be promoting tattoo products, you can have a website name like "realtattoos.com"

Hope that doesn't sound too awkward! It is just an idea.

You will also need to host your website unless you design your own website. Bluehost is a popular website hosting service.

To make navigating your site easy, you may need to use some tools like WordPress. WordPress is a very effective and common tool which is used to manage contents on a website.

With WordPress, one can easily add new content and also delete old content from a website. Although it is laid out in a blog-like manner, it is still an effective tool to capture your sales. (Note that the layout of a blog is not fitting for a sales page).

Looking at the sales pages of competitor affiliates can really give you an idea of what your sales page should look like. Personally, this has worked for me. I made it a serious task to find those who worked online, particularly those whose earnings had skyrocketed within a short period of time.

Are you wondering why we're talking so much about your sales page?

It is too important to be overlooked. Your sales page is what ultimately determines how well you sell on Clickbank. If your sales page is good, with a nice pitch, you will attract buyers; but if it is the other way round, then buyers won't be interested in your products.

Did you know that words can aid your sales?

Those who have successful sales also have great content with which they persuade buyers. If you do not have great content, then your chances of convincing a buyer are very small. Getting good content is not so difficult. You can employ the services of a competent copywriter to help you write content that sells.

Learn from Professional Affiliates

Now that you are getting acquainted with the procedures involved in promoting a product, you may also need to garner more information from top affiliates. They are always willing to guide young affiliates to become successful like them.

Looking to create a sales page that sells?

Visit a number of sales pages, especially those who have recorded great sales over time. From these pages, you can find out what you think attracts people to them, or the kind of content they use to persuade people to buy from them, and many other things that you can lay hold on.

You can also try to view things from your own perspective: Create your sales page and ask yourself honestly, if you are convinced to buy a product from that page assuming the page wasn't yours. If you answer honestly, you will know the next step to take – whether to create another sales page or to improve on the existing one.

What should my sales page look like?

Generally, a sales page will look like a review by someone who has used a product at one time or the other. It will appear to have solved a particular problem that the person had. So, you can engage your readers in a convincing way.

However, we have to be clear on something here...

We are dealing with humans, right? You don't want to sound too 'over the top' or your potential buyers will feel you are trying to scam them. Try sounding like someone who is giving an honest review of the product.

If the product has a disadvantage, mention it – though not emphatically; otherwise, you will ruin your chances of ever selling the product. Why would you want to promote a product with too many flaws anyway?

Let's consider promoting a product under "Computing & Internet" category: You are promoting an eBook that teaches Java programming. No matter how good the book is, it would obviously be impossible for that book to completely capture the entire scope of Java programming language. Therefore, an appropriate review can look like this:

I was just getting started with my programming career and I was in need of materials to sharpen my skills. A friend told me about this one and I decided to give it a try. I found the book very helpful for programmers at different levels. Although there are not many visual aids for better understanding, I became a professional programmer because of things I learned in this book.

I strongly recommend this book for any individual who is passionate about programming and wants to improve their skills.

You should also include a salesy picture that best fits the context.

Another way to present your sales page is to review more than one product. You can review two or more products and name your sales page after something that connects all the products together.

Use a modern rating system for the products. The most common rating system is the 5-star method... Thereafter, list the products in order of their importance, that is, the most relevant product should rank number one while the others follow in the same succession.

Another way to market products on your sales page is to review two or more products (preferably of the same category). You can then give distinct reviews of these products. Let's use a practical example here:

Assuming you review three products under the "Health & Fitness" category. The first product is an eBook that teaches you how exercising can help to prevent sugar-related diseases; the second teaches exercising as a way to keep fit and strong; while the third teaches daily exercising as a way to be motivated.

Here's a sample of how you can review the three products:

First product:

This product contains vital information about how exercising can combat sugar-related diseases. It also contains videos of exercises you should do every day to stay healthy. This is not suitable for body-builders

Second product:

How distinctive do you want your six pack to be? This guide has videos and an eBook to show you the most effective ways to build your muscles. However, it does not cover the scope of healthy living...

Third product:

Did you know that daily consistent exercising can help you to be motivated? This eBook shows you how exercising can help you achieve your life goals. It doesn't place any emphasis on health anyway.

People have often asked me if it is necessary to buy all the products they are reviewing, and my answer to them is this: Yes and No

Why I say Yes...

Buying and using the products help you get first-hand information and experience about the product. As a result, you will be able to provide honest reviews that stem from a true knowledge of the product.

Why I say No...

When your sales begin to expand, it may become quite difficult to buy all the products you review or you'll spend too much. However, there's a way you can get around it.

Some merchants provide adequate information about their products. Let us consider an example of a product page about dogs by SitStayFetch. The product package contains an eBook and a lot of photos.

Here's what the merchant says about the product..

> ...I designed *SitStayFetch* to be the easiest system to follow on the market today for learning how to train your dog and change its behavior. It is jam-packed with information, including how to solve over 25 dog behavior problems, real-life case studies, the best dog training techniques, unlimited dog behavior consultations with the SitStayFetch team, loads of photos that will boost your learning AND step-by-step instructions... all within one instantly downloadable package.

You can GO AHEAD with a review of this product without buying or using it. Just review based on what the merchant has said about it:

• Learning how to train your dog and change its behavior

• How to solve 25 dog behavior problems

• Best training techniques

• Unlimited consultations with the SitStayFetch team

• Instant download of full package, and more...

The merchant gave even more information. Look at the picture below.

Need to stop your dog from trying to fight with other dogs? Learn the best ways to break up dog fights and **prevent them from ever happening again.**(page 84-86)

Want to know how to curb your dog's aggressiveness? Learn six powerful strategies for training aggressive dogs. (pages 60-72)

Did you know that your dog may not know why you are trying to correct him? Learn how to **make him understand**. This will remove the frustration and rapidly increase the speed of your dog's learning. (Page 37, plus further communication strategies provided throughout)

All the secrets of professional dog trainers are revealed, and best of all are easy to apply! Stop wasting hundreds of dollars (chapters 103, 201, and 301)

Does your dog require urgent dog house training? Learn the dog house training techniques you must know that get the **fastest results**, whether you keep your dog indoors or outdoors. (chapters 103, 203, 302 plus house training bonus book)

Sick of having your dog race out the front door? Read my book and you'll never have to worry about this again. (page 116)

Got a dominant dog? We teach you how to deal with him. (chapters 201, 202, plus bonus book)

Separation anxiety getting you both down? Find out about the best ways to make it go away. (pages 143-144 and Separation Anxiety case study: pages 145-146)

Hate having your dog jump up on you? Learn six simple techniques to stop him jumping up on you ever again! (pages 141-142 and Jumping case study: pages 143)

Neighbors getting annoyed with your pet's constant barking? Maybe he doesn't bark enough? Apply these advanced techniques so that your dog knows when and where it's appropriate to bark. (pages 56, 86-89, 127-128)

Here is another Clickbank product to consider – No nonsense muscle builder. This merchant also provided adequate information about his product. So you do not need to buy and use the product. Instead, you can read his description and use it to review the product on your sales page.

✓ **Discover the #1 most critical muscle building ingredient you can't grow without.** More important than training, nutrition, supplementation and even more than anabolic steroids! Don't do this and you have **no chance** of building your perfect body!

✓ **Side step the top 20 ways to screw up in the gym.** By simply avoiding these suicide training techniques that 98% of trainees do, you will make twice the gains in half the time! You'll be training smarter... not harder and the results will blow your mind.

✓ **Maximize the top 9 little known anabolic secrets for hyper-drive muscle gain.** Every single one of these principles MUST be executed to build even one pound of muscle. You will not casually discover these rules on any website or in any fitness magazine. Once you learn to exploit each one consistently, your growth will explode! Bodybuilders at your gym will be coming to YOU for advice! You're no longer on the outside looking in.

✓ **Gain 10 pounds in 2 weeks (Did I stutter? This is no lie!)** With my mass gaining plans, you will eat to grow huge. I tell you exactly what to eat and how much to eat, to ensure you get maximum growth. I guarantee this is unlike any eating plan you've ever heard of and I GUARANTEE you SERIOUS muscle gains. Yes... 10 pounds of solid muscle in 2 weeks! Imagine the instant change in your appearance. Stay out of sight for 2 weeks and when you return, you're like the "Incredible Hulk!"

✓ **Learn exactly how to absolutely optimize 7 of your body's most powerful muscle growth and fat burning hormones.** These are the same hormones bodybuilders and professional athletes shoot with 5 inch needles into their asses. I'll show you how to NATURALLY switch your body's own anabolic hormones into overdrive. You will maximize your workout and bulk up fast.

✓ **Steal my closely guarded 52 week weight training routine.** The same routine "the rich" pay me boatloads of cash to teach them! Let me take you by the hand and show you EXACTLY how to pair your muscles. How many sets you must do. How many reps. How much weight. How much rest. And most importantly... how fast to move the weight and when to change the program. You have NEVER seen this program in ANY fitness magazine or on ANY bodybuilding website. The results will make you look for every opportunity to take your shirt off in public!

This merchant gives a list of techniques that he has compiled to help you build your muscles quickly and effectively.

From the merchants' product pages, you can already determine what the benefits of using a product are, as well as the disadvantage of using the product. Therefore, you can skillfully create an honest review of the product and highlight both the positive and negative sides to the product.

Note: Don't forget to attach your hoplink (remember we learned how to create that in chapter three of this book) to every product you're reviewing on your sales page, so that you can get compensated adequately for your hard work.

Still on the sales page...

If you cannot afford to host a webpage to use as your sales page, you can access some free tools which will help you to achieve your goals. Squidoo is an online service that allows you to create free web pages called lens. It is used by many affiliates who cannot afford hosting a web page at the moment too. Visit www.squidoo.com to get started.

Like every other free domain service, your site will have the name squidoo on it.

Here's what I mean: If your website name is healthyproducts, the address will be www.healthyproducts.com/squidoo.

I would consider this to be even better than many other free domains which use formats like www.healthyproducts.***.com. (where *** is the domain name)

Another thing about Squidoo is that it doesn't feature many ads that may have nothing to do with your reviewed products, which sometimes can be a distraction. If you can afford a website, I suggest you get one; however, Squidoo is not a bad idea if you can't afford a domain.

You can check out www.weebly.com and www.blinkweb.com for free web hosting and template designs. These free domains have paid upgrades if you want to continue using them, and enjoying the best of their services. They also help you avoid the services of a graphic designer.

Some affiliate programs will include website plug-ins to help you completely build your website and give you links to discount webhosting services. **Check out the Bonus Quick Start Guide.**

In the next chapter, we are going to consider how to generate traffic to your sales page so that you can make money steadily from the sales of products on your sales page.

Chapter 6 - How Will People Find Your Site?

Creating a sales page with a very marketable product review is not all there is to making sales as an affiliate marketer. You still need to drive traffic to your page so that you can enjoy the maximum inflow of potential buyers to your sales page consequently increasing your chances of earning much.

In this chapter, you will learn the most effective way to drive traffic to your website. My advice for you is this: Pay close attention!

There are different methods, both legal and illegal, that people use to drive traffic to their website. One of the most common methods is the use of Google AdWords.

Google AdWords

The use of Google AdWords is a quite big topic, so I suggest you get relevant information and study materials from www.google.com/adwords. After visiting the site, navigate to their learning center. They have many lessons that are worth studying. Within two days, you should be able to set up campaigns correctly with AdWords.

Google AdWords is fun and easy to learn, but it requires devotion and practice to master, like anything else that you master. The old adage that practice makes perfect is especially true here.

When you use Google AdWords, you can create ads that Google will post on other websites so that as people browse the internet, the ads can capture their interest, and they will probably click them. You will then be charged every time a person clicks on one of your ads.

Here's one tip that you will find useful as an affiliate marketer: for every review page you create, ensure it is not a one-page website. Google will charge you more for each keyword phrase that you bid on if they discover that your website is a low quality website – they consider one-page websites to be low quality websites.

The safest practice, therefore, is to create about five or six other pages and link to them.

The pages you create can include your privacy policy, a contact me form, as well as reviews and information about your products such as "how to lose 50 pounds in 2 weeks", "how to become a better programmer in ten simple steps", "how to download iTunes to your Apple products", and so on, depending on the kind of products you are promoting.

Another tool people use to promote their products and drive traffic to their sales page, other than Google AdWords is Article Marketing.

How does this work, you ask?

You will have to write a fairly short article, preferably between 300 and 600 words for an article directory site. The article you write for them should be helpful, informative, related to your affiliate product, and of course accurate in terms of grammar and spelling. If you can't do a thorough writing job, you had better hire the services of a writer.

For example, if you are selling an eBook titled 20 foods to eat for breakfast from the "Health & Fitness" category, you could write about 10 reasons why it is necessary to eat breakfast.

I have said this before: we are dealing with humans here, so you need to be smart with your articles. If your article is too promotional, the article directory may reject your article. In fact, many of these directories do not appreciate any sales copy.

Does this sound like Guest posting to you? It probably is a form of guest posting.

What is the importance of writing these articles, you ask?

First, you will be able to include a resource box or a bio box, depending on the directory you're using. Using this box, you can link either to your sales page or directly to the product merchant's page. Just describe your link with something not too salesy.

Something like this: Tired of thinking about best food combinations for your breakfast, click this link for detailed information on that.

[Please note that not all directories will allow you to post your hoplink on their page; so it is best to know the terms and conditions of each article directory before using their services. Nevertheless, every article directory will allow you to post links to your own website in the articles].

Article directories that you can write guest posts on include the following: ezinearticles.com, goarticles.com, buzzle.com, isnare.com, articlecity.com, associatedcontent.com, articledashboard.com, selfgrowth.com, articlealley.com, easyarticles.com, articlerich.com, article99.com, bestsyndication.com, articlesbin.com, americanchronicle.com, articlecafe.net, and many more.

If you want to stand a better chance of getting many people to click your links, then you need to write as many articles as possible. If you hate writing, hire freelancers who are willing to do it at very low rates. You can find them on freelancer sites like upwork.com, guru.com, fiverr.com, freelancer.com, and so on.

Another effective way to promote your affiliate products is to find forums that are relevant to your products and post helpful comments. Try as much as possible to avoid sounding promotional. Then include a link to your web site in your signature. Your signature is created when you sign up to that forum.

Be original, helpful and provide useful information in your comments on forums. Don't appear to be promotional or you may be ignored or totally banned. It's the safest thing to do if you want members to pay attention to your comments.

Ensure your signature blends with your comments. For instance, on internet marketing sites, don't ask for best ways to make money online knowing that your signature file and link suggest that you own a "make money online" site.

Many people have fallen into this trap and lost their credibility. Therefore, you need to be calm and not overly excited so you can make the most of such forums.

The final method of generating traffic that I will mention here is Viral Marketing. It is a more organized and less tricky (so to say) way to promote your products.

What you need to do is to write a short report that is relevant to the product you want to promote.

For example, if you are promoting a programming language eBook. You could write a report, say four pages, with a title like best programming languages and their relevance and give it away for free on programming-related web sites and forums. However, ensure that you have attached your affiliate link (hoplink) to the product you are promoting.

Whether you are promoting a product in the "Computing & Internet" category, or in the "Business to Business" category, (or any other category) this method works!

Note: People often assume that just gaining access to information is all that is required to experience change. That is actually a wrong idea! What will bring about the change you desire is how you practice the tips and methods in this eBook.

Get to work immediately!!!

CHAPTER 7 - CONCLUSION

At this point, you are now on your way to earning well over $100 dollars. The maxim at the beginning of this book says, how to make your first $100 online. But that is quite conservative because you can earn so much more than $100 online per day if you put in the required work and effort.

A great number of people have left their conventional jobs to focus on affiliate marketing, and it has really paid off for them. Many engineers, doctors, lawyers, teachers, have laid aside their profession, partially or totally, to join the onrush of successful affiliate marketers, and now have great success stories to share.

My advice to you is to not see this book as the angle that will meet your financial needs, but merely as an opportunity to learn valuable information that will actually solve your financial problems when you practice the things in it.

This book contains all that you need to excel in affiliate marketing on Clickbank, either as a beginner or as a growing affiliate marketer. We have covered helpful topics such as introducing Clickbank as a profitable affiliate marketing platform, choosing the right product on Clickbank, creating a hoplink, creating a converting sales page and then driving traffic to your sales page.

Are you still sitting there reading this and not doing anything? You could be making money right now. You can use the extra cash to build your dream house or buy your dream car! You may even be able to quit your conventional job.

Take action!

Share with your friends and family if you found this eBook useful.

It was great sharing this information with you and I hope that it helps you achieve all of your financial goals. I hope you had fun reading!.

ABOUT THE AUTHOR

IQ Press, Inc. is a small publishing company dedicated to providing access to educational materials primarily in small business start-up and development. Their mission is to bring the reader useful information that can be implemented with a small capital outlay and generate income streams for the reader to implement.

We hope you enjoy these reports and that they will help improve your life.

Check out more great reports at:

www.IQPress.org

REFERENCE MATERIALS

Other books you may enjoy to help you on your journey:

Affiliate Marketing for Beginners. *Have you heard about affiliate marketing but not quite sure if it's real or really works? This definitive guide will lay out the ins and outs of this interesting field. Filled with tips and hints, it also has information on what to look out for.*

Affiliate marketing truly can be started with very little money and has the potential for great rewards. Simple to start with the right guidance, affiliate marketing seriously reduces the risk in starting your own business. Imagine a business with little investment, no inventory, no customer service, no shipping and handling and no risk! Further it can grow to replace your current income and still be operated as a part-time operation. All you need is the enclosed information and you're ready to start.

Affiliate Marketing Secrets: *You did become an affiliate marketer to become rich, right? OK, so now what? Start here and learn how to take your fledgling affiliate marketing company to the next step. This report is packed with secret tips and tricks to help you grow your company quickly. After all, your goal is to add customers and new products quickly and expand your business without taking on more risk.*

In this short read you will find dozens of ideas to help move your company forward. Not a bunch of theoretical ideas but actual tested tips and techniques to move you towards your goal quickly.

Finding the Best Affiliate Products to Promote: *How do I find the best products to sell? Now that you know about affiliate marketing and its great income potential, how can you choose what product(s) to promote? You want one with high demand but not too much competition. You need to choose the category, the product, the venue, the program, etc… That's quite a lot for a new company owner! We can help. This guide will walk you through all these decisions and keep you from getting in a bad place with a product that has poor sell-through.*

Affiliate Marketing and Success Systems: *This report is a compendium of tips and ideas to help keep you on track with your affiliate marketing business. You want an automatic money machine? We'll show you not only how to grow but also to get that growth on autopilot! With a few simple programs you can get the company to generate a continuous income stream. That's why you went into this type business, right?*

Using this report will turbocharge your results and help you simply and effectively grow your sales. Bring in a constant stream of new customers and new products to offer your existing customers for a generous income. You could even quit your job if you wanted! Imagine all that free time while still enjoying a great income.

Available exclusively at: www.IQPress.org

www.ingramcontent.com/pod-product-compliance
Lightning Source LLC
LaVergne TN
LVHW052125070326
832902LV00038B/3946